Cape Cod Journey

Photographs by

KATHARINE KNOWLES

BARRE PUBLISHERS   **BARRE, MASSACHUSETTS 1966**

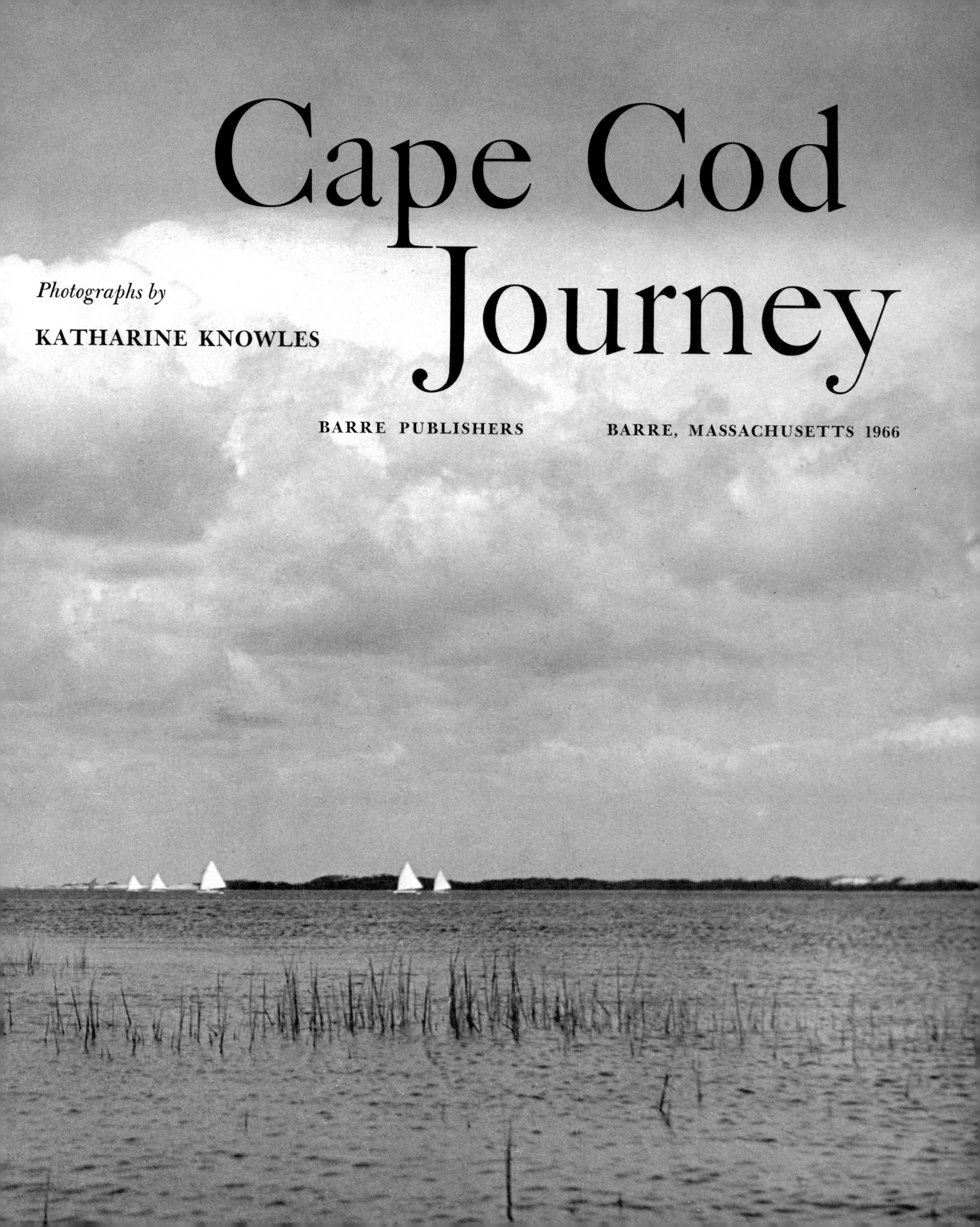

INTRODUCTION

CAPE COD is unusual in its wealth of scenery and history; the task of making a photographic impression of it was a delightful one. This book's purpose is not to give a complete picture of the Cape, but to capture its essence — the charm and atmosphere of this incomparable land jutting into the Atlantic from Buzzards Bay.

The Cape is a land of salt marshes and sand, inland lakes and rivers, historical museums and summer resorts. But, ultimately, life on the Cape is governed by the Atlantic. Along both the Bay-side and the Oceanside are strung fishing villages, old whaling towns, the home ports of sea captains, awesome stretches of dunes, magnificent white, sandy beaches.

The "Route of History," (6A) is the route of the camera traveling east. Through the lovely towns and quiet villages of Sandwich, Barnstable, Yarmouth, Dennis, Brewster, Orleans, then on Route 6 to Eastham, Wellfleet, Truro, and Pro-vincetown at the farthest tip of the Cape. For the most part, the return is along Route 28 through Chatham, Harwich, Hyannis, Oyster Harbors, Falmouth and finally to the old trading post of Aptucxet along the canal at Bourne.

The establishment of the Cape Cod National Seashore Park has ensured the preservation of the beauties of the Cape. Its intent is "to conserve the scenery and the natural and historical objects and wild life therein, and to provide for the enjoyment therein of the same in such a manner and by such means as will leave them unimpaired for the enjoyment of future generations."

This is the journey, a fleeting glimpse of beautiful Cape Cod.

KATHARINE KNOWLES
Cambridge, 1966

IN MEMORY OF
AUGUST BELMONT
FEBRUARY 18, 1853 – DECEMBER 10, 1924
WHOSE VISION, INITIATIVE, AND INDOMITABLE
COURAGE MADE POSSIBLE THE FIRST COMPLETE
CONSTRUCTION OF
THE CAPE COD CANAL
CONNECTING BUZZARDS BAY AND CAPE COD BAY
WHICH WAS OFFICIALLY OPENED FOR TRAFFIC
JULY 29, 1914.
FROM HIS MATERNAL GRANDFATHER
COMMODORE MATTHEW CALBRAITH PERRY
HE INHERITED A WARM ALLEGIANCE TO THE INTERESTS
OF NEW ENGLAND AND HIS DEEP CONCERN FOR
THOSE WHO GO DOWN TO THE SEA IN SHIPS.

*A freighter in the Cape Cod Canal on
its way to the open sea.
Two bridges spanning the Canal
provide entry to the Cape.*

Lake Wequaquet from the mid-Cape Highway.

A tempting spot for a picnic.

SANDWICH

above: Enduring houses of the early settlers line Main Street.

right: Uplands, an early eighteenth-century house.

above: An unusual saddle-shaped stone marks the grave of Edmond Freeman, a Sandwich founder, and his wife, Elizabeth.

right: The Town Hall and the Congregational Church built in Greek Revival style during the Quaker period — 1834.

*above: The Sandwich Glass
Museum preserves a prized
collection of glass.*

*right: Close-up of the rare
pattern glass housed in
the museum.*

*left: The seventeenth-century
Dexter Grist Mill faces Shawme
Lake. Shawme swans and
their young among the reeds.*

The gracious old homes of Sandwich give an air of dignity and peacefulness.

*following pages: The Hoxie House, built in 1637, is said to be the oldest house
on Cape Cod. It stands on the banks of Lake Shawme.*

above: The oldest Quaker Meeting House in America.

top left: the sloping saltbox roof of the Hoxie House.
bottom left: Graves in this burying ground date from as early as 1663. Across the lake is the Hoxie House.

Fresh-water fishing on one of the Cape's many lakes and ponds.

*West Parish Meeting House, circa 1717, is the
oldest Congregational Church in America.*

BARNSTABLE

above: The unusual anchor cross of our Lady of
          Hope Catholic Church in Barnstable.

top right: Sign of the wrought iron craftsman.

bottom right: A Revolutionary marker.

West Parish Parsonage, once the home of
Lemuel Shaw, Chief Justice of the
Supreme Court.

Deserted light at Sandy Neck.

*Boats bob in a squall at
Barnstable Bay.*

Storm clouds over Barnstable Bay.

*A lonely house
faces the marshes
on the dunes
at Sandy Neck.*

above: The Church of St. Mary.

right: Daffodils in St. Mary's churchyard.

top left: Sturgis Library, built in 1645, is the oldest library building in the country.

lower left: The Crocker Tavern dates from 1754.

left: *The steeple of the Unitarian Church.*

below: *The cannons in front of the gray granite County Court House were brought by ox-team from Boston during the War of 1812.*

YARMOUTH

Marshes in the afternoon sun.

following pages: Cummaquid

above: The Parnassus Book Shop.

left: Old Town Pump at Yarmouthport.

right: The Winslow Crocker House (1780).

below: The Colonel John Thatcher House (1680).

above: The "Route of History," Highway 6A, passes through Yarmouth.

top right: The 1721 House.

right: The Village Green: On the right is the old Yarmouth-Dennis Historical Society.

above: Indian mounds in a pine grove.

right: Over the marshes at the Town Landing, Bass Hole.

below: Sandy Sides Beach at Dennis Pond.

Scargo Hill Tower.

*Scargo Lake and Massachusetts Bay
from the top of Scargo Tower.*

The celebrated Dennis Playhouse.

Scargo Lake.

left: The original mill on this site, built in 1660, was one of the first water powered grist mills in America and the first woolen mill (1680). The present mill, erected in 1874, operates during the summer. The upper story is a museum.

right: The herring run in this stream near the mill.

below: The Drummer Boy Museum.

*Packet ships on their way to New York once stopped at the river
landing bordering Meeting House Pond, in East Orleans.*

Rock Harbor was a commercial and maritime center in the early days, but now (following pages) sport and commercial fishermen use the harbor.

EASTHAM

First Encounter Beach. Here on a sand dune overlooking Cape Cod Bay is a marker commemorating the first encounter of the Pilgrims and Indians.

The oldest workable windmill on the Cape, and, below, Salt Pond, with its inlet to Nauset Bay.

WELLFLEET

Dunes on Chequessett Neck stretch for miles.

The chapel of St. James the Fisherman, designed by architect Olav Hammerstrom.

Wellfleet from the harbor shore.

Wellfleet Town Hall is a close replica of the original which was destroyed by fire.

following page: Provincetown from the Town Wharf.

above: The Pilgrim Monument.

top center: Commercial Street with flags flying on Festival Day.

top right: A waterfront studio.

bottom center: The Town Square on Festival Day.

bottom right: Cottages with their backs to the morning sun.

PROVINCETOWN

A fishing boat pulls alongside the wharf with its morning catch.

TRURO

*Highland Light
stands on a
one hundred
and fifty foot
bluff. Under
ideal weather
conditions, its
light can be
seen from fifty
miles at sea.*

top left: Corn Hill — Salt meadows, green marsh grass and cat o' nine tales.

bottom left: Cottages in Truro.

right: U. S. Coast Guard Station at Highland Light.

An Interpretive Shelter built by the National Park Service houses explanatory material about the surrounding area.

In the far distance is the "Fo'castle", where Henry Beston wrote
"The Outermost House."

Nauset Light.

*Aunt Lydia's Cove at
Pleasant Bay.*

A prize catch is weighed.

CHATHAM

The Old Grist Mill of Chatham, built in 1797 by Captain Benjamin Godfrey.

Fishing at Oyster Pond River.

above: *Oyster shacks along the Oyster Pond River.*

The Old Chatham Railroad Station is now a museum.

left: In Harwich Center is
Pine Grove Academy, the
first maritime academy
in the country.

below: Town Library and
District Court. On the right
is the Old Powder House
in use from 1780 to 1864.

right: The Congregational
Church.

*Friends Meeting House, South Yarmouth.
The town was once known as
Friends Village.*

Bass River looking upstream.

HYANNIS

left: The Church of
St. Francis Xavier where
the late President Kennedy
and his family worshipped.

right: St. Andrew's by the
Sea at Hyannis Port.

below: Looking out over the
Port Golf Club and
Nantucket Sound.

OYSTER HARBORS

Crosby Yard, where the popular catboats were built.

*This Post Office at Cotuit
reveals a touch of
American Gothic.*

Old Indian Church (1684).

right: Mashpee Pond.

FALMOUTH

above: *The Village Green and these
eighteenth century homes
were once lived in by sea
captains and patriots. The house
with the balcony is the Historical
Museum, built in 1790.*

right: *A bit of New Seabury.*

NEW SEABURY

Exact reproduction of Aptucxet Trading Post — birthplace of American commerce in 1627.